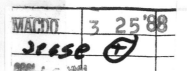

Skills On Studying

HELP IS ON THE WAY FOR:

Grammar

Written by Marilyn Berry
Pictures by Bartholomew

ℂℙ CHILDRENS PRESS ®

CHICAGO

Childrens Press
School and Library Edition
ISBN 0-516-03280-1

Executive Producer: Marilyn Berry
Editor: Theresa Tinkle
Consultants: Terie Snyder and Theresa Tinkle
Design and Art Direction: Abigail Johnston
Typesetting: Curt Chelin

So your teacher wants you to work on your **grammar.**

Hang on! Help is on the way!

If you are having a hard time
- understanding the parts of speech,
- understanding the parts of a sentence,
- speaking and writing correct English...

...you are not alone!

Just in case you're wondering...

...why don't we start at the beginning?

What Is Grammar?

Grammar is a set of rules that serve as a guide to help us use our language correctly. The rules are a standard for us to follow so that we all speak the same way.

Two Kinds Of English

Almost everyone uses two different types of English. In formal situations such as in school or public speaking, we use a formal type of English called *standard English*. At these times, we follow the rules of grammar strictly. When we are with friends or in an informal setting, we often use *informal English*, which "bends" some of the rules of grammar.

Why Is Grammar Important?

Learning the rules of grammar can help you in all areas of your schoolwork and your communication with others. You will also find that good grammar will continue to help you in many ways throughout your life.

You may not realize it, but you have been learning the rules of grammar since the day you began to speak. You would be surprised at how much you already know. Now you need to learn the finer points. It's really not very hard if you take it slowly and one step at a time.

Step One:
Mastering The Parts Of Speech

All the words in the English language can be divided into eight categories. These categories are called *parts of speech*. The parts of speech are

- nouns
- pronouns
- verbs
- adjectives
- adverbs
- conjunctions
- prepositions
- interjections

In order to understand grammar, you need to understand and master the parts of speech.

Nouns

The word "noun" means "name." That clue will help you remember what a noun does. It *names* a person, place, or thing.

You can usually identify a noun by putting "the" in front of it. If this sounds correct, it is probably a noun. Here are some examples of nouns:

Pronouns

A pronoun is a word that takes the place of a noun. For instance, you can say
- "she" instead of "Jill."
- "they" instead of "clowns."
- "it" instead of "book."

Pronouns can add variety to your speech.

Verbs

A verb is a word that expresses action such as "fly," "cook," and "laugh."

You can usually identify a verb by putting "to" in front of the word. If it makes sense, it is probably a verb.

A verb can also express a state of being. An example is the different forms of the verb "to be" such as "is."

Adjectives

An adjective is sometimes called a "modifier" because it can modify or change the meaning of a noun or pronoun. Adjectives can answer questions such as "which?," "what kind?," or "how many?" about a noun or pronoun.

An adjective usually gives additional meaning to a word to make it more precise.

Adverbs

An adverb can also be called a "modifier" because it can modify or change the meaning of three different types of words:

- A verb—He ran *quickly*.
- An adjective—The cake is *very* good.
- Another adverb—I ate *too* much.

Adverbs can answer questions such as "how?," "where?," or "when?"

Conjunctions

A conjunction is a word that is used to join together words or groups of words. Some conjunctions are "and," "but," "yet," "so," "for," "or," "nor." A conjunction can connect

- Words—Craig *and* Brian live next door.
- Phrases—Let's go down the block *and* across the street.
- Clauses—Pets are fun *but* they are also a lot of work.

Prepositions

A preposition is a word that shows direction or location. Some prepositions are "in," "around," "under," and "from." A preposition is usually part of a phrase that describes a word in the sentence. The preposition links the phrase to the word it is describing.

In the sentence

The dog in my bed is asking for trouble.

the word *in* is a preposition and *in my bed* is a prepositional phrase.

Interjections

An interjection is a word that expresses emotion or excitement. Interjections are often followed by an exclamation mark. For example:

Wow!   *Ouch!*   *Whew!*

Some interjections are used as filler words and are followed by a comma. For example:

Oh, I think we should go.

This has been just a simple overview of the eight parts of speech. Each part has its own set of guidelines. Every time you discover a new guideline, it will help you to improve your grammar. Write the guidelines down as you learn them, so you don't forget them.

Step Two:
Mastering The Parts Of A Sentence

Once you have learned the eight parts of speech, you need to learn how those parts can be used in a sentence. There are six major parts of a sentence:
- The subject
- The predicate
- The direct object
- The indirect object
- The predicate noun
- The predicate adjective

But first, let's review the definition of a sentence.

The Complete Subject

The subject of a sentence is the person, place, or thing that the sentence is talking about. The subject consists of a noun or pronoun and its modifiers. To find the subject of a sentence, ask yourself "Who or what is the sentence about?"

In the sentence

> The brand new skateboard was glistening in the store window.

the subject is *the brand new skateboard.**

* The simple subject is *skateboard*.

The Complete Predicate

The predicate is the action part of the sentence. The predicate consists of the verb and its modifiers. To find the predicate of a sentence, ask yourself "What is the subject doing?" or "What is happening to the subject?"

In the sentence

> The dog ate all of its food.

the predicate is *ate all of its food.* *

* The simple predicate is *ate.*

The Direct Object

The direct object is the part of the sentence that receives the action of the verb. The direct object is a noun or a pronoun.

In the sentence

> She bought the toy.

the direct object is *toy* because that is the thing that was bought.

The Indirect Object

The indirect object is the part of the sentence that receives the direct object. The indirect object is a noun or pronoun and usually comes before the direct object in the sentence.

In the sentence

> She bought the dog a bone.

the indirect object is *dog* because it receives the direct object, which is *bone*.

The Predicate Noun

The predicate noun is the part of the sentence that *renames* the subject. It is a noun and usually follows the verb in the sentence.

In the sentence

My dog is my friend.

the predicate noun is *friend* because it renames the subject, which is *dog*.

The Predicate Adjective

The predicate adjective is the part of the sentence that *describes* the subject. It is an adjective and usually follows the verb in the sentence.

In the sentence

My dog is spoiled.

Spoiled is the predicate adjective because it describes the subject, which is *dog*.

A Word About Sentence Diagramming

A sentence diagram is a figure that is used to identify the parts of a sentence and how they are related to each other. For those who are visual learners, diagramming can be a valuable tool. You may want to learn more about sentence diagramming. Here are the two basic patterns you would use:

Step Three:
Mastering The Types Of Sentences

There are three basic types of sentences:
1. The simple sentence
2. The compound sentence
3. The complex sentence
Learning how to use all three types of sentences will help you with both your speaking and your writing skills.

The Simple Sentence

A simple sentence consists of one subject and one predicate. For example:

The dog hated the cat.

one subject   one predicate

It is important to note that a simple sentence can have two or more nouns as a subject or two or more verbs, but it will still be a simple sentence. For example:

The dog and cat teased and fought with each other.

The Compound Sentence

A compound sentence is really two simple sentences that are joined together by a conjunction such as "and," "but," "or," "nor." Each part of the sentence has equal weight and could stand alone. For instance:

The dog tried to become friends, but

simple sentence   *conjunction*

the cat would not listen.

simple sentence

The Complex Sentence

A complex sentence has at least two parts:
- a main clause and
- one or more dependent clauses.

The clauses are joined together by a conjunction such as "after," "although," or "if." For example:

The dog and cat went their separate ways
_____
main clause

    after   the fight was over.
   ————   ————————————

conjunction   *dependent clause*

Step Four: Gathering Tools To Improve Your Grammar

There are so many rules of grammar that it would take you a long time to learn them all. In fact, few people need to memorize all the rules. However, you can gather a few tools that will serve as a reference for your questions about grammar. They are

- a dictionary,
- a complete book of grammar, and
- your own personal grammar notebook.

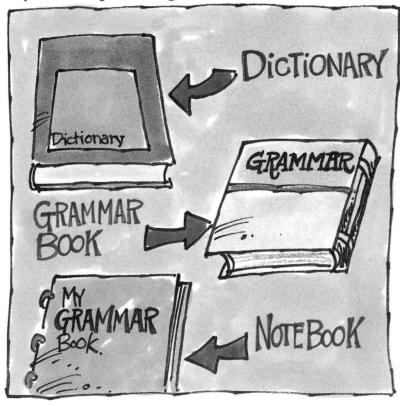

The Dictionary

You may not realize it, but a dictionary can answer some of the questions you may have about grammar. Besides giving the meaning of a word, a dictionary can
- tell you which part of speech the word is,
- show you other forms of the word, and
- show you how the word can be used in a sentence.

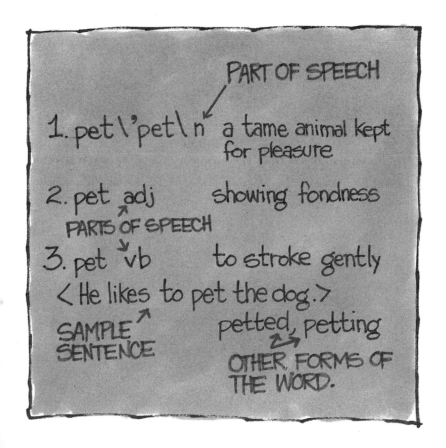

A Book Of Grammar

There are many books of grammar available in book stores and in libraries. Some are written for people your age. These books usually are not meant to be read like a novel. They are meant to be used as reference books to answer your questions as they arise. Ask your teacher or librarian to help you choose a grammar book that will be easy to use.

Your Own Personal Grammar Notebook

It is a good idea to keep a notebook just for facts that deal with grammar. Some things to include in your notebook might be

- rules of grammar,
- sample sentences that illustrate the rules,
- lists of pronouns, irregular verbs, prepositions, and conjunctions,
- common grammatical mistakes.

Step Five:
Learn From Common Mistakes

There are several common grammatical mistakes. As you discover these mistakes, write them down in your notebook and try not to fall into the same trap twice. Here are a few to get you started.

Mistake #1: Irregular Verbs

If the three major tenses of the verb "talk" are

	talk	talked	talked

and of the verb "drop" are

	drop	dropped	dropped

then the tenses of the verb "bring" must be

	bring	bringed	bringed

Unfortunately, that's not true.
We have several irregular verbs like "bring" in English, and the only way to learn them is to memorize them.

Mistake #2: Misusing Pronouns

Many people do not know whether to use "me" or "I" in the following sentence:

Would you give Brent and _____ some cookies?

They have similar problems with other pronouns as well.

Here is a good rule to follow: "I," "he," "she," "we," "they" are used as subjects, predicate nouns, or predicate adjectives. "Me," "him," "her," "us," "them" are used as objects.

Mistake #3: Subject And Verb Disagree

A singular subject needs a singular verb. For example:

The boy has a black eye.

singular subject   *singular verb*

Some people get confused when the subject is more complex such as

One of the boys _____ a black eye.

Don't be fooled by the word "boys."

Mistake #4: Subject And Pronoun Disagree

A common mistake is to put a plural pronoun with a singular subject. For example:

A person is lucky when they have a pet.

singular subject   *plural pronoun*

The correct way is:

A person is lucky when he or she has a pet.

singular subject   *singular pronouns*

or

Mistake #5: The Misplaced Modifier

Sometimes a modifier that is in the wrong place can change the meaning of a sentence. For instance, in the sentence

> He gave the paper to the teacher
> that was wrinkled.

it sounds like the teacher was wrinkled. The modifier is in the wrong place. The sentence should read:

Mistake #6: The Split Infinitive

An infinitive is a verb form that includes the word "to" such as "to go," "to finish." An infinitive is split when an adverb is placed between the "to" and the verb, for example:

to suddenly *go*   or   *to* quickly *finish*

You should move the adverb to a better place in the sentence:

to go suddenly   or   *to finish* quickly

Mistake #7: The Run-On Sentence

If you want to join or combine two or more sentences into one sentence, you need to add conjunctions. If you don't, you will have a run-on sentence. This is a run-on sentence:

> I don't want to go to bed I'm not tired I want to watch T.V.

A better way to say it would be:

Mistake #8: The Sentence Fragment

An incomplete sentence is called a sentence fragment. A sentence fragment does not give the reader enough information. A common sentence fragment begins with the word "because." For instance:

Because we were hungry.

A better way to say it would be:

We were hungry.

You could also give the reader more information:

A Helpful Hint
The next time someone corrects your grammar,
ask the person to tell you
• what you said wrong,
• the correct way to say it, and
• the rule behind the correction.
Then, put the rule in your grammar notebook
and try to remember it.

WARNING!

If you follow the suggestions in this book, your grammar will probably improve and...

...so will your grades!

THE END

About the Author
Marilyn Berry has a master's degree in education with a specialization in reading. She is on staff as a creator of supplementary materials at Living Skills Press. Marilyn and her husband Steve Patterson have two sons, John and Brent.